Humpty Dumpty

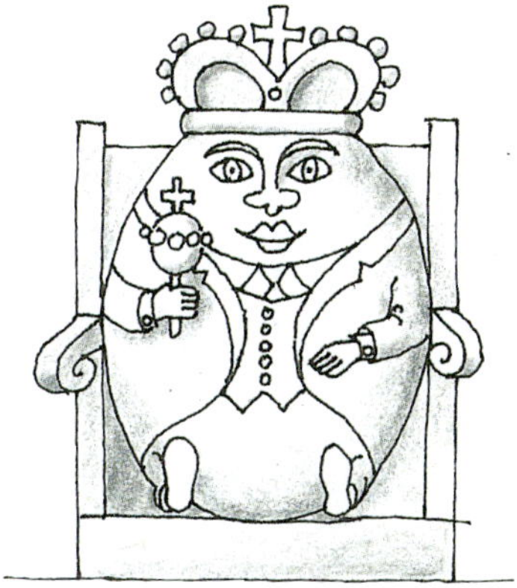

Illustrated by Alan Peacock

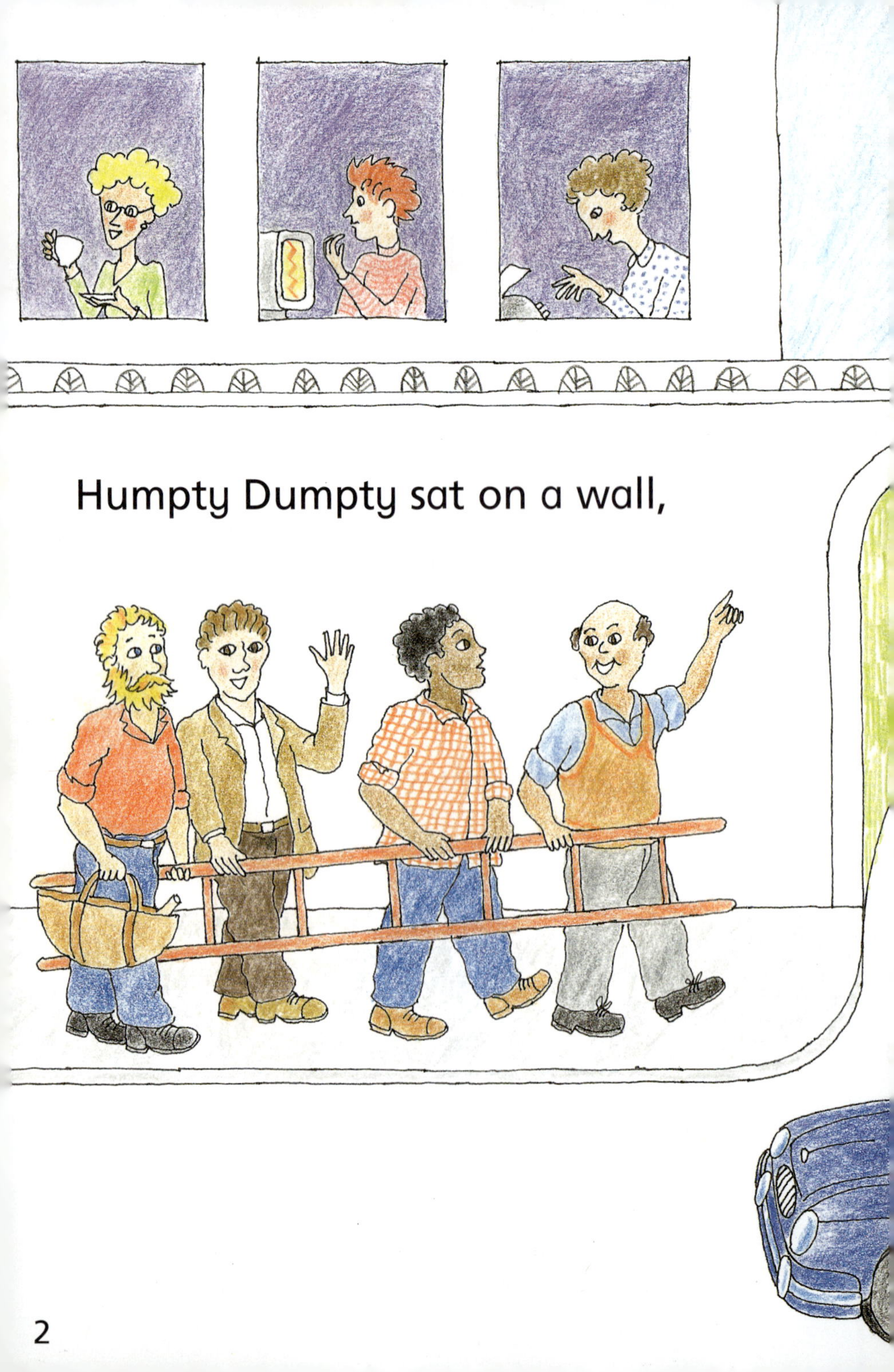

Humpty Dumpty sat on a wall,

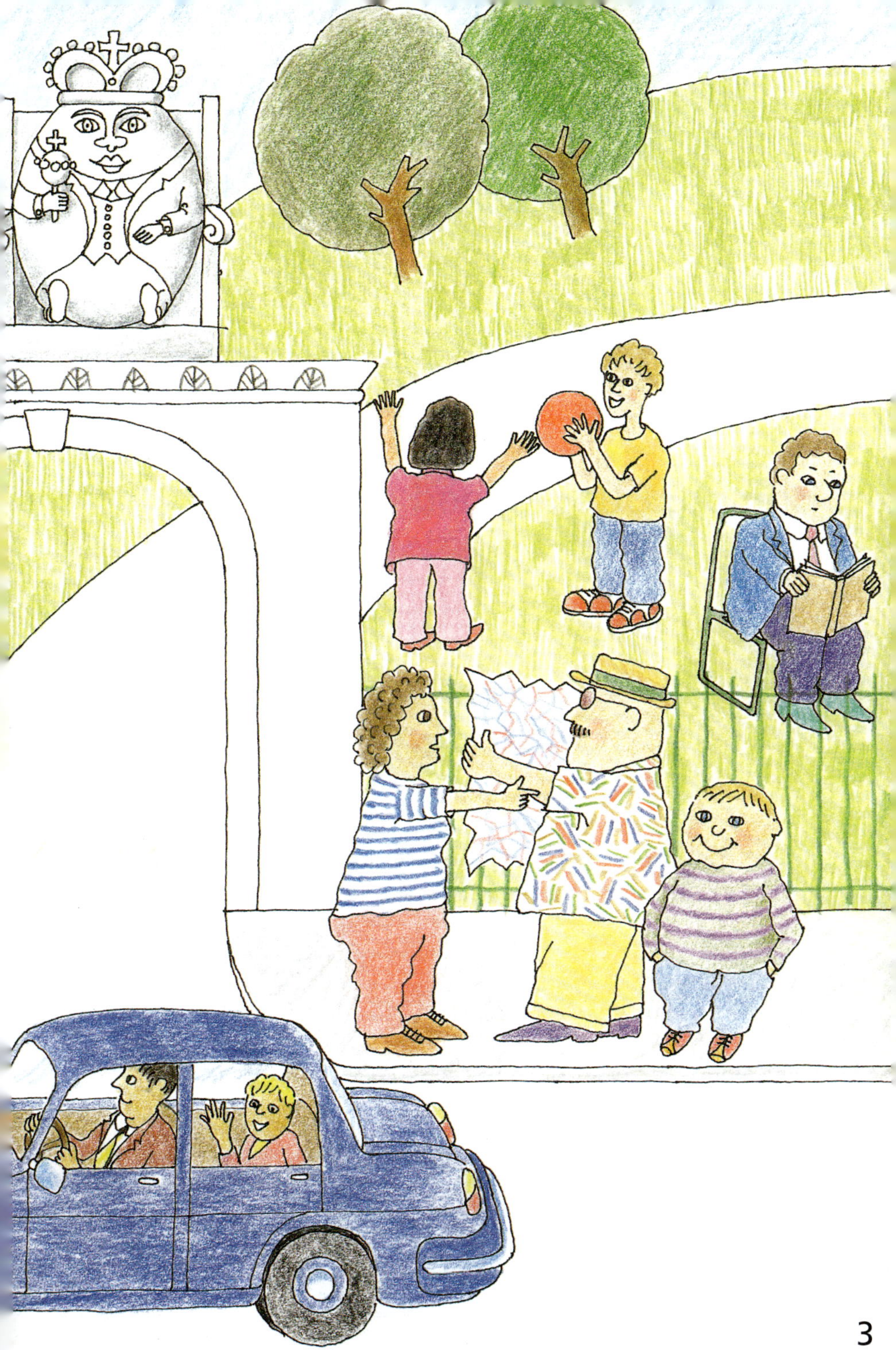

Humpty Dumpty had a great fall.

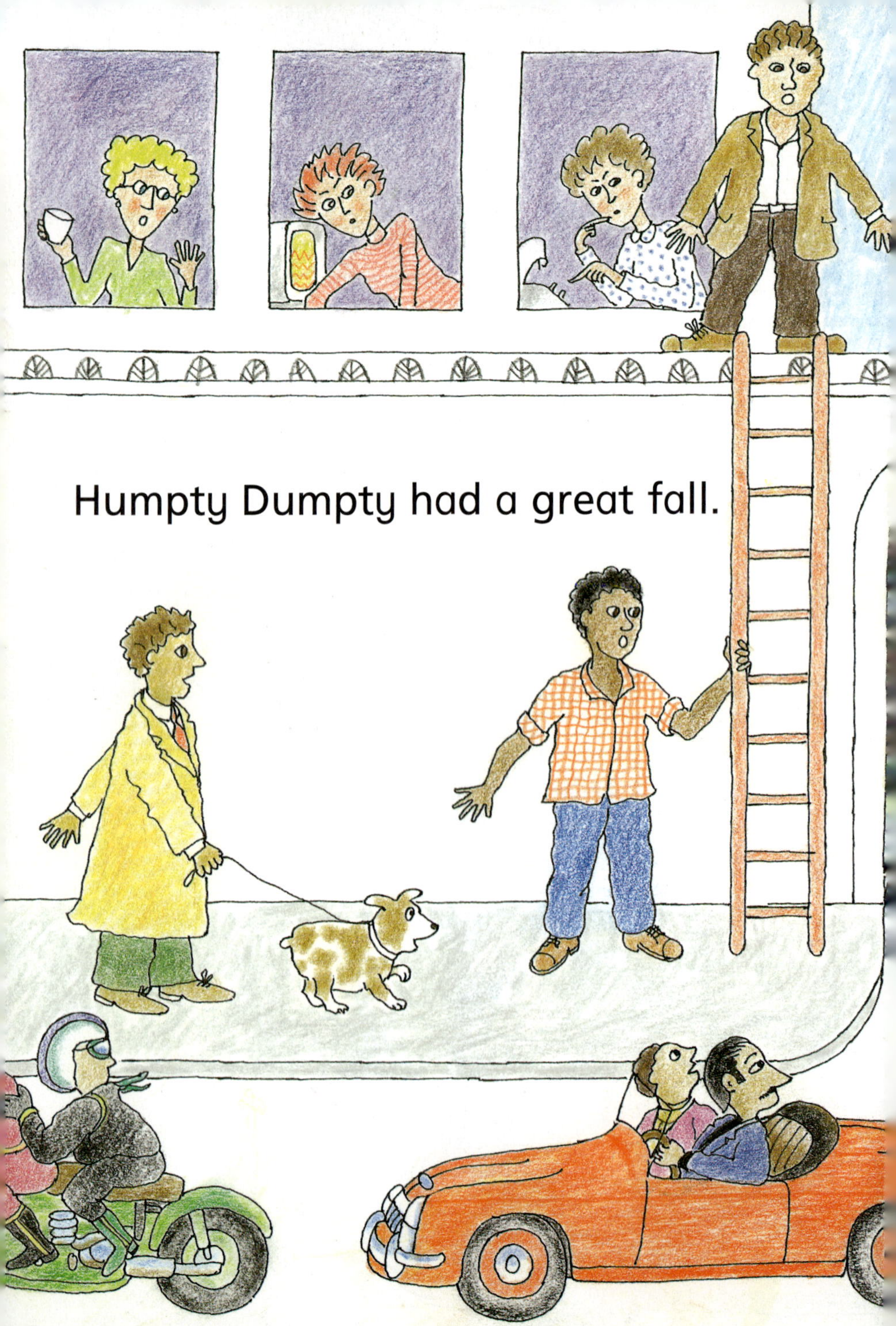

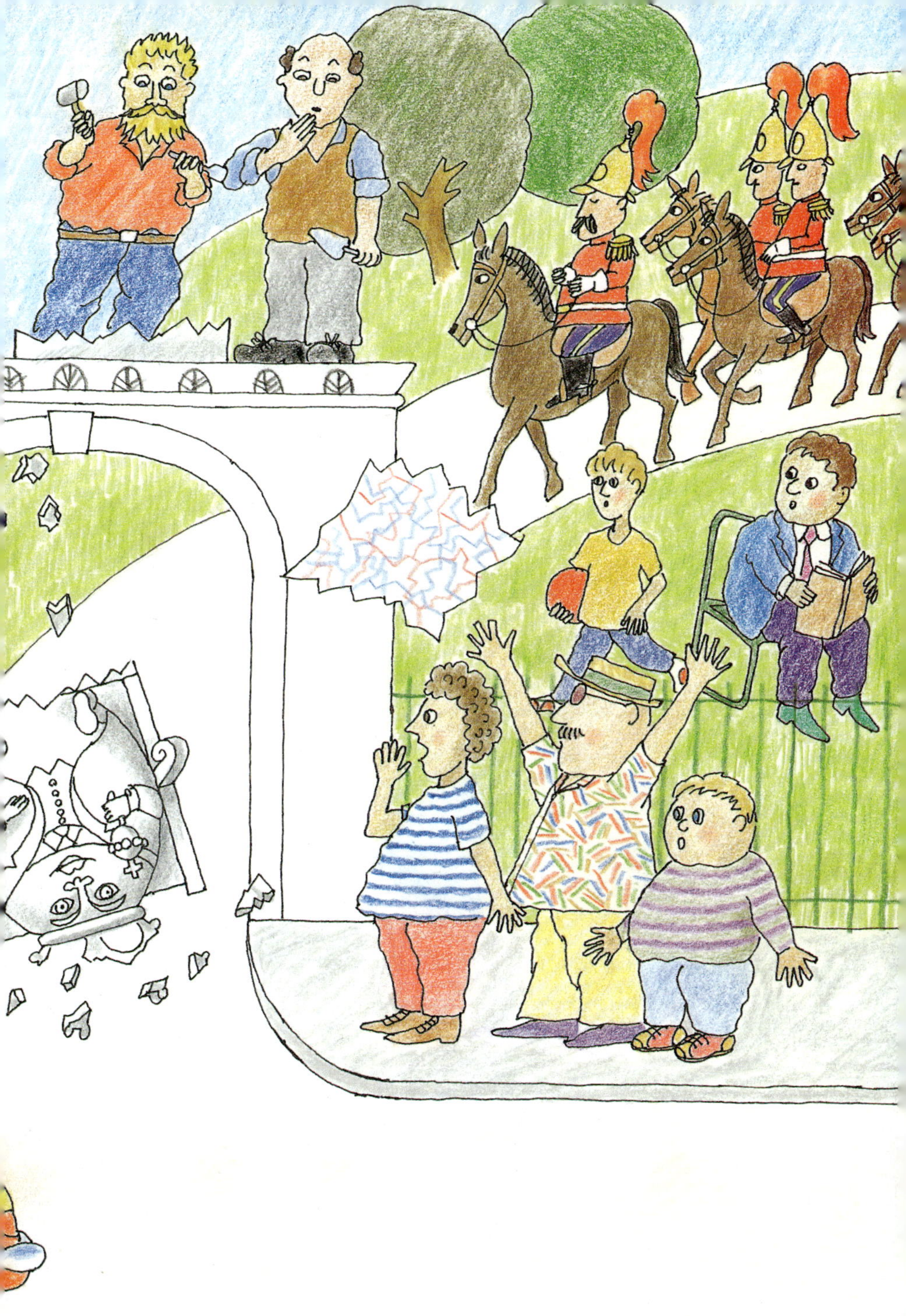

All the king's horses and all the king's men

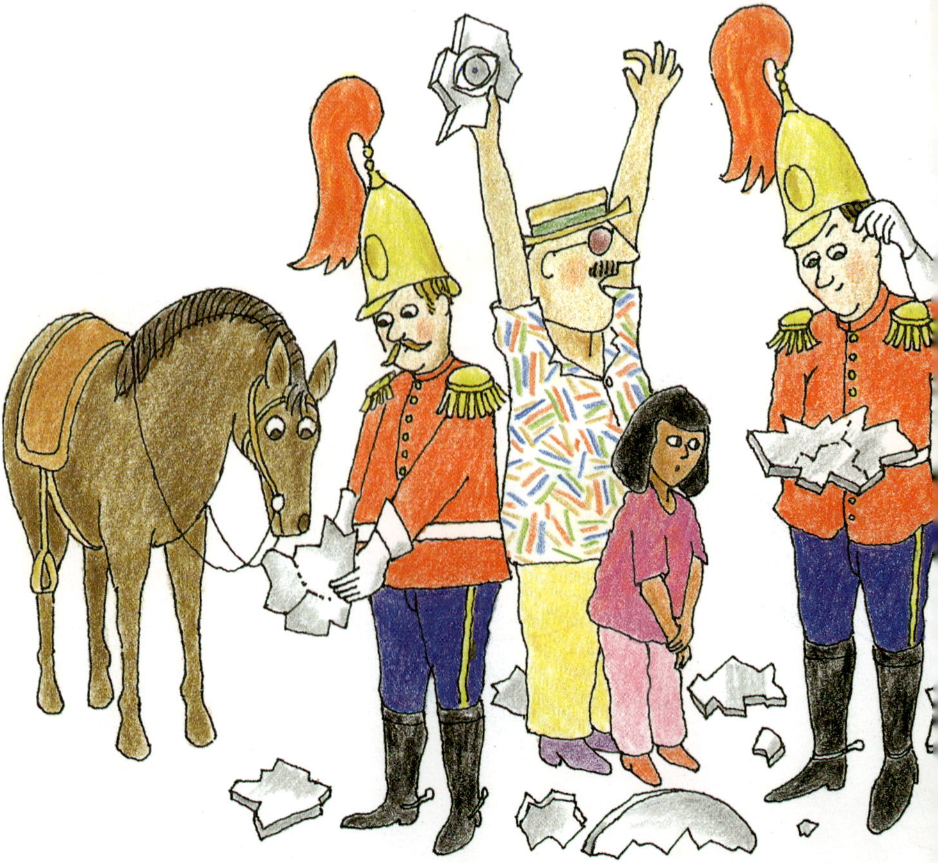

couldn't put Humpty together again.

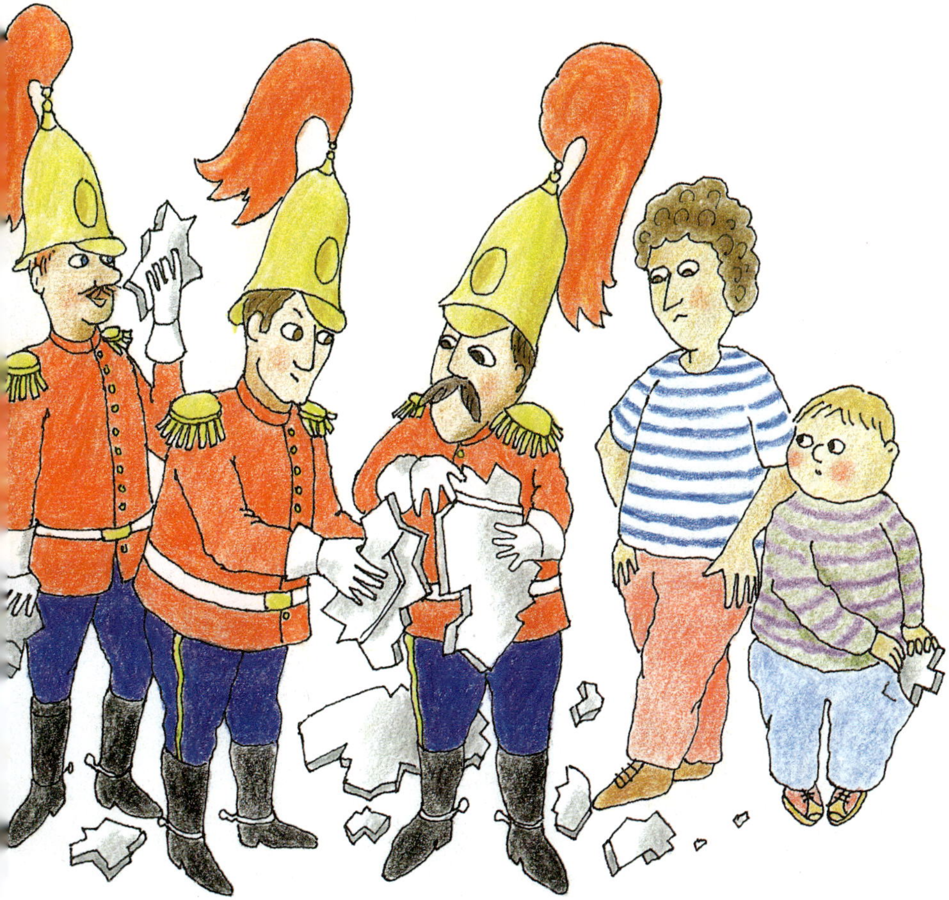

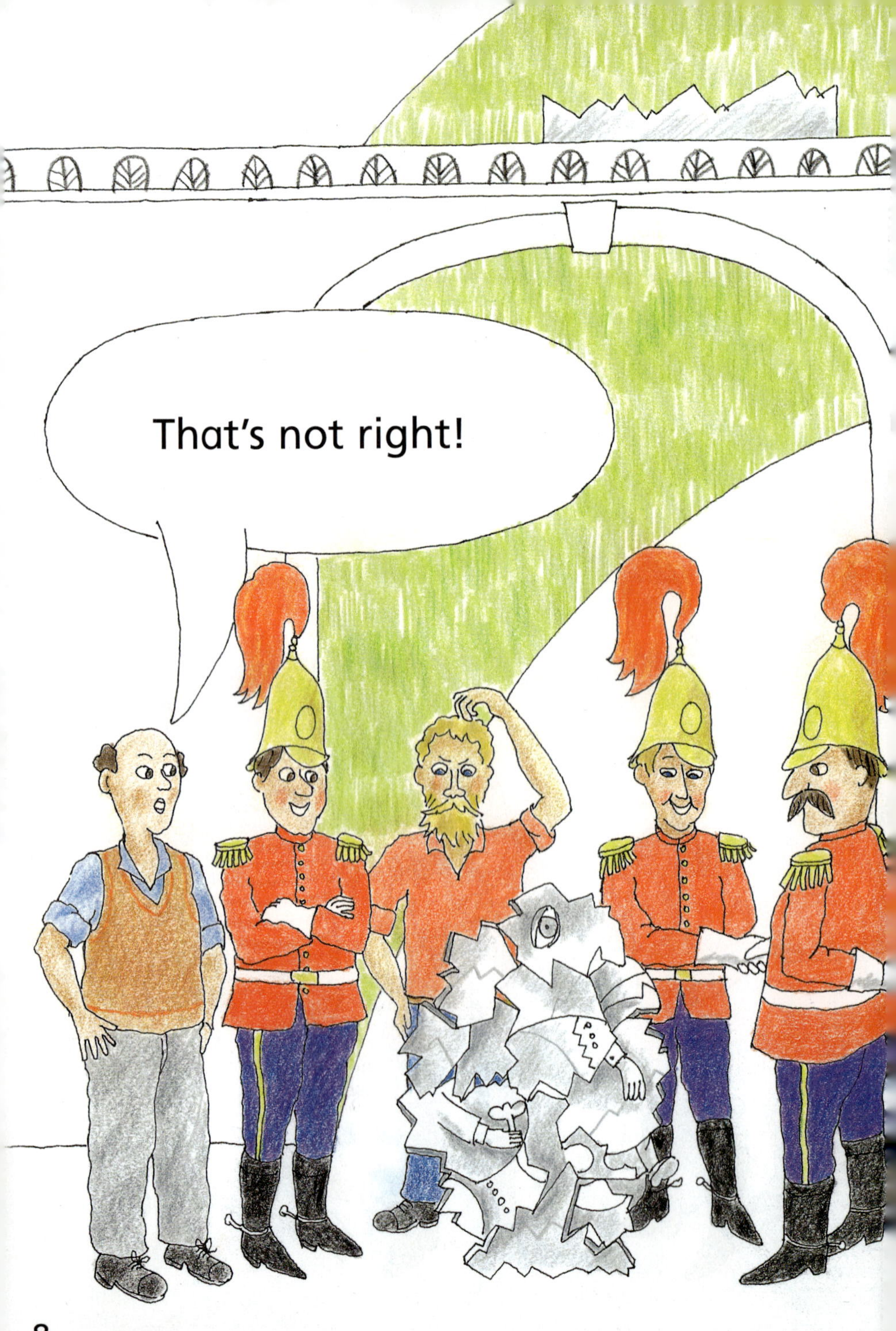
That's not right!